AIR

Troll Associates

AIR

by Keith Brandt

Illustrated by Ray Burns

Troll Associates

Library of Congress Cataloging in Publication Data

Brandt, Keith, (date)
   Air.

   Summary: Explains the qualities of the air that we breathe
and of the air in the layers of the atmosphere, and
briefly discusses gravity and air pressure.
    1. Air—Juvenile literature.   2. Atmosphere—Juvenile
literature. [1. Air. 2. Atmosphere] I. Burns, Raymond,
1924-   ill. II. Title.
QC161.2.B68   1984   551.5   84-2608
ISBN 0-8167-0130-X (lib. bdg.)
ISBN 0-8167-0131-8 (pbk.)

10   9   8   7   6   5   4   3   2   1

What is it you can't see, hear, feel, taste, or smell but surrounds you all the time? It's the air! Just as fish live in a sea of water, you live in a deep sea of air. You walk through it. Balloons and planes fly in it. There is air around every bird and insect, every tree and flower, every hill and valley. Air fills the deepest caves and covers the highest mountain peaks.

Every living thing in the world needs air. From the moment we are born until the moment we die, we must have air. Awake or asleep, we breathe air all the time. The same is true for birds and bees, worms and fleas, walruses and whales.

Even an unborn chick in its eggshell must have air. The eggshell may seem to be solid, but it really has hundreds of tiny holes. Air comes in through these holes and is used by the unborn chick.

Since air is invisible, how can you prove it exists? Put a straw into a glass of water and blow into it. You'll see bubbles form, rise to the surface, and pop! These are air bubbles.

You can also prove there is air by using a rubber balloon. Before it's inflated, the balloon is limp and shapeless. But as soon as you blow into it, the balloon starts to grow round and firm. What makes this happen? Air.

Even in ancient times, people knew that air was important, but they didn't know why. Then, about 200 years ago, scientists began to study air. The first laboratory experiments were done by an English chemist named Joseph Priestley.

First, he put a burning candle in a jar and covered it. Soon, the candle went out. Then, he put a mouse in another jar and covered that. After a while, the mouse died.

Next, Priestley tried a different experiment. He put a mouse and a healthy green plant into a covered jar. This time the mouse stayed alive. But soon after the plant was removed, the mouse died.

Joseph Priestley learned some very significant facts from his experiments. He learned that a burning candle must have air or it will go out...that a mouse must have fresh air or it will die...and that the plant somehow kept the mouse alive. What he didn't know was why these things happened.

Today we know a lot more than Priestley knew. In the 200 years since his studies, scientists have learned that air contains gases. One of these is oxygen. Oxygen is the gas a candle needs to burn. Oxygen is what mice—and all animals—need to stay alive.

When Priestley's mouse used up all the oxygen in the airtight jar, it died. Scientists have also found that green plants give off oxygen. And that is why the plant kept the second mouse alive.

Plants and animals work together in the use of air. Animals breathe in oxygen and breathe out another gas called carbon dioxide. Green plants take in carbon dioxide. Then the plants use carbon dioxide and sunlight to grow. At the same time, they give off the oxygen animals breathe in. If plants stopped making oxygen, our world would soon be lifeless!

If you could take a bucket of air and cut it into five equal parts, one part would be oxygen. Almost all of the other four parts would be a gas called nitrogen. And the tiny bit of air left over would be gases called carbon dioxide, neon, argon, xenon, krypton, helium, hydrogen, ozone, and water vapor.

All of the air between the Earth's surface and outer space is called the *atmosphere*. The atmosphere is made up of several layers, like a layer cake. As you go up, each layer has less oxygen than the one below.

The layer we live in, the bottom one, is the *troposphere*. The gases that make up the troposphere are very active. The air moves up and down, the winds blow, the clouds build up, drift away, and swirl in the sky. All the clouds we see are in the troposphere.

The troposphere is not a very thick layer. At the North and South Poles, it is only about the same height as Mount Everest, the tallest mountain in the world.

At the equator, the belt that goes around the middle of our planet, the troposphere rises about twice as high as Mount Everest. The troposphere is thicker at the equator because the air is warmer there, and warm air rises. The air at the poles is very cold, and so it doesn't rise as high.

Wrapped around the troposphere is a layer called the *stratosphere*. This layer is about 20 miles, or 32 kilometers, thick. The air in the stratosphere is dry and almost always clear. In this clear, cloudless layer the sky is a velvet black and stars glow brightly day and night.

The upper part of the stratosphere is the *ozone* layer. Ozone, the only gas in the air that has an odor, is very important to life on Earth. The ozone layer is like a huge shield that blocks most of the sun's ultraviolet rays. Ultraviolet rays can destroy living cells. Without the ozone shield, life on Earth probably could not exist.

The next layer is called the *mesosphere.* It is about the same thickness as the stratosphere, but it is much colder. The coldest air in all the atmosphere is found at the top of the mesosphere.

The *thermosphere* is next. It is the thickest of all the layers, and it stretches far into space. It is made up of the *ionosphere* and the *exosphere.*

The thin air of the ionosphere crackles with electrically charged particles known as *ions.* Radio waves from Earth hit the ionosphere and bounce back to Earth. This makes it possible for you to hear a radio program broadcast in another part of the world.

The exosphere is above the ionosphere. It contains very little air. Beyond it, there is nothing but outer space.

What keeps the air around the Earth from drifting off into outer space? The same thing that keeps every boy and girl, car and truck, ant and elephant on the ground. The answer is gravity.

Gravity is the force that pulls things toward the center of the Earth. Anything

that has weight is affected this way by gravity. And each particle of air has weight. A particle of air does not weigh very much. But the weight of all the air in the atmosphere is very great. The air presses down on the Earth. This is called *air pressure.*

Scientists have measured air pressure. They tell us that at sea level, there are fifteen pounds of pressure on each square inch of Earth, or about one kilogram per square centimeter. At the top of a high mountain the pressure is noticeably less than at sea level.

Air is pressing on you all the time, but you aren't aware of it because you also have air *inside* your body. And the pressure inside your body is the same as the pressure outside. So a perfect balance exists.

There *are* times when you can feel a change in air pressure. You can feel it while flying in an airplane or riding in a fast-moving elevator. The pressure inside your body remains the same, but the outside pressure is lower. Your ears may start to hurt or clog. But breathe in the outside air, and you'll equalize the pressure and feel normal again.

Air pressure plays a big part in making our weather. Masses of air move around the Earth all the time, pushing in all directions. When a mass of cold air forms it always presses down. When a mass of warm air forms it always rises.

As an air mass moves it picks up water

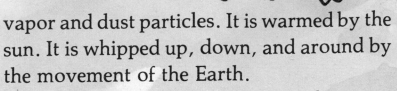

vapor and dust particles. It is warmed by the sun. It is whipped up, down, and around by the movement of the Earth.

After clouds become heavy with water, rain or snow will fall on the Earth below. In March, chill winds blow; in July, soft, warm breezes whisper through leaves and grass. Hot-cold, wet-dry, stormy-calm...the weather is always changing.

The ocean of air around us carries information of all kinds. It also brings us the warmth of the sun, the scent of a flower, and the sound of a drum. Without air, the drum would *bang!* But you wouldn't hear it. When a drumstick hits a drum it makes the air

around it vibrate. These vibrations reach
your ear, and your ear turns them into
sound. If you lived in a vacuum—a space
without a trace of air—there would be
nothing to carry the vibrations, and there
would be no sound.

Without air there would be no sound, no rain, no you, no me. Without air, the Earth would be cold and dry, silent and lifeless. But air is all around us. We may not be able to see it or hear it. We may not be able to touch it, taste it, or smell it. But it is there. Air is everywhere. And it is truly our most precious resource.